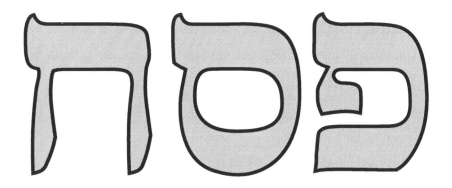

This Pesach activity book belongs to:

_____

Find more unique Jewish notebooks, planners, coloring books, and journals created for you by ©Jewish Chai Life: amazon.com/author/jewishchailife

Exodus from Egypt

יציאת מצרים

PHARAOH FORGOT YOSEF

Why did pharaoh act against the Jewish people?
Why did he make them into slaves?

משה

Moshe (Moses)

משה   משה   משה   משה   משה

משה   משה

מרים

Miriam

מרים אמרים אמרים אמרים

מרים אמרים

אהרן
Aharon

אוהרון אוהרון אוהרון

אוהרון אוהרון

PESACH IN A MAZE

Pharaoh's daughter is on her way to the Nile. Help her find the way!

FIND 10 DIFFERENCES!

TORAH VERSES WORTH KNOWING

וַיִּשְׁמַע אֱלֹקִים אֶת־נַאֲקָתָם
וַיִּזְכֹּר אֱלֹקִים אֶת־בְּרִיתוֹ אֶת־אַבְרָהָם
אֶת־יִצְחָק וְאֶת־יַעֲקֹב:

And God heard their crying,
and God remembered His
covenant with Abraham,
with Isaac, and with Jacob.

וישמע אלקים את נאקתם

ויזכר אלקים את בריתו

את אברהם את יצחק

ואת יעקב

PESACH IN A MAZE

Help Moshe, Tzippora, Gershom, and Eliezer reach Egypt!

PESACH WORDS WORTH KNOWING

Color, read aloud, trace, copy, and - if you can, memorize!

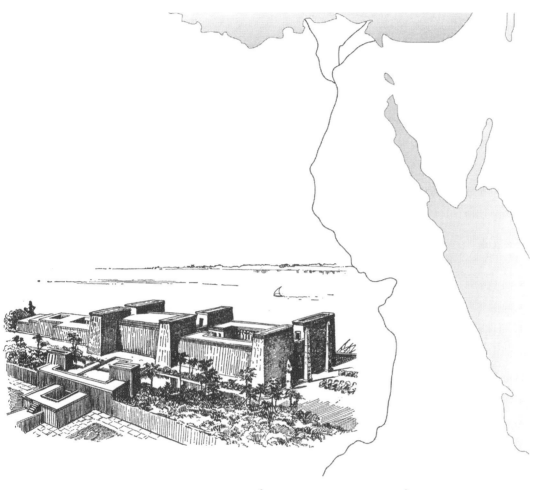

(mitzrayim)

Egypt

מִצְרַיִם

AT THE ROYAL PALACE
OF THE PHARAOH

What do you think the throne room of the pharaoh's palace
looked like? Draw it below:

PESACH IN A MAZE

Moshe has lost one of his sheep. Help him find it!

GOD'S MESSENGER

God chose Moshe to be the leader and a prophet.
What did he tell the people of Israel when he returned to Egypt?
What do you think were the Hebrew's thoughts?

OVERCOMING HARDSHIPS

Moshe had a speech impediment he worked hard to overcome.
Draw and write about two hardships you overcame.

_____

_____

_____

_____

_____

_____

_____

_____

_____

_____

_____

_____

_____

_____

_____

_____

PESACH WORDS WORTH KNOWING

Color, read aloud, trace, copy, and - if you can, memorize!

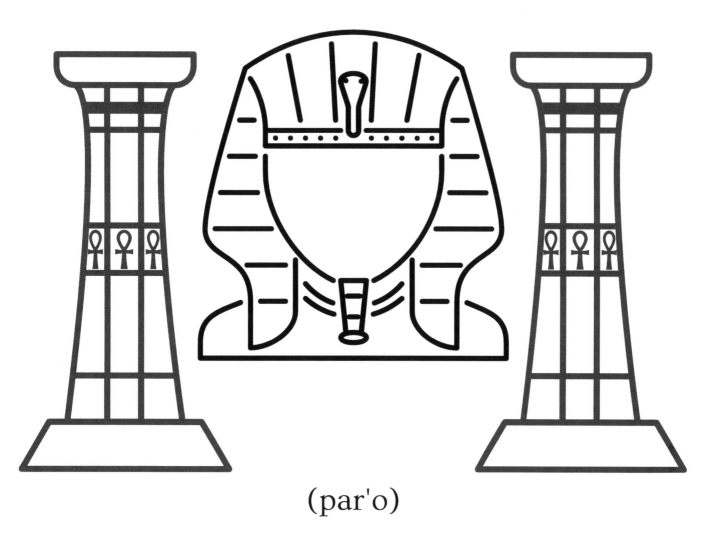

(par'o)

Pharaoh

פַּרְעֹה

PESACH IN A MAZE

Pharaoh has lost his crook and flail - the royal insignia of the Egyptian rulers. Show him the correct path to them.

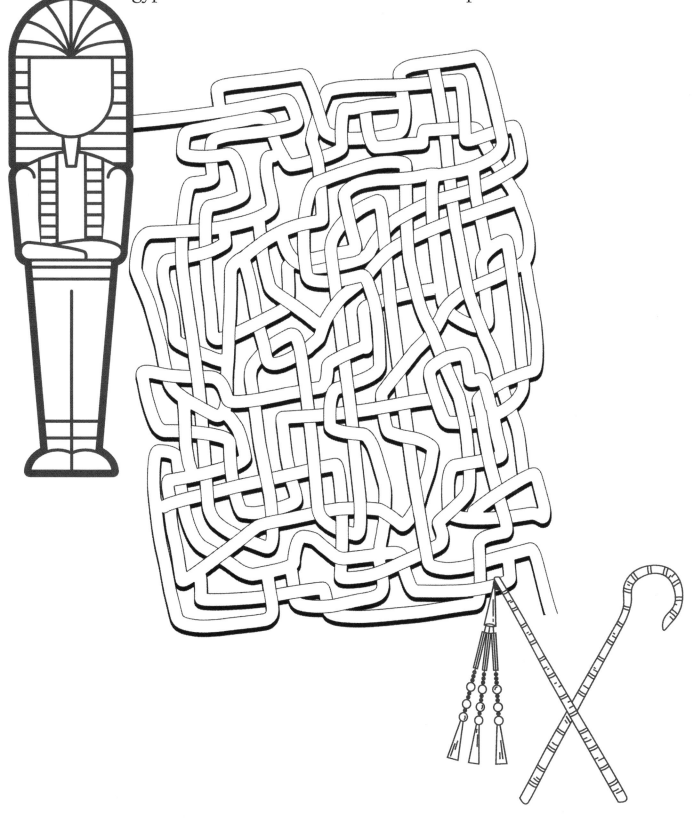

TORAH VERSES WORTH KNOWING

כֹּה־אָמַר ה' אֱלֹקֵי יִשְׂרָאֵל
שַׁלַּח אֶת־עַמִּי
וְיָחֹגּוּ לִי בַּמִּדְבָּר:

"Thus says the LORD,
the God of Israel:
Let My people go that they
may hold a festival for Me
in the wilderness."

כֹּה אָמַר ה' אֱלֹקֵי יִשְׂרָאֵל
שַׁלַּח אֶת עַמִּי וְיָחֹגּוּ לִי
בַּמִּדְבָּר

THE EGYPTIAN PLAGUES - MAKKOT

Draw what each of the first nine plagues looked like - inside the appropriate cypher.

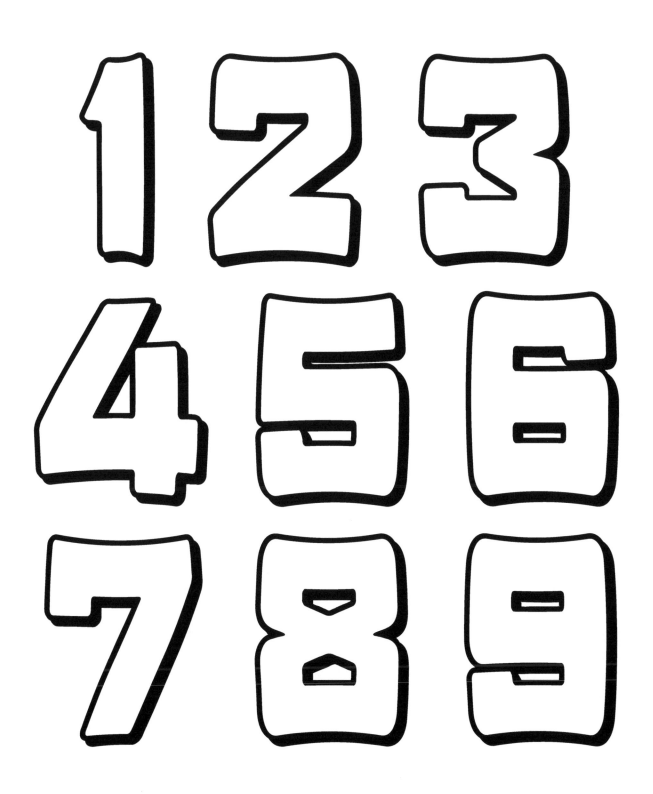

CHAMETZ OR NOT A CHAMETZ?

Circle and color products which we can eat during Pesach. Avoid
chametz - all (processed) food made with grains
that had the time to ferment.

MISSING LETTERS

Fruits are some of the best Pesach foods, being naturally chometz-free! Write down the missing letters of the Hebrew alphabet and color all the delicious fruits!

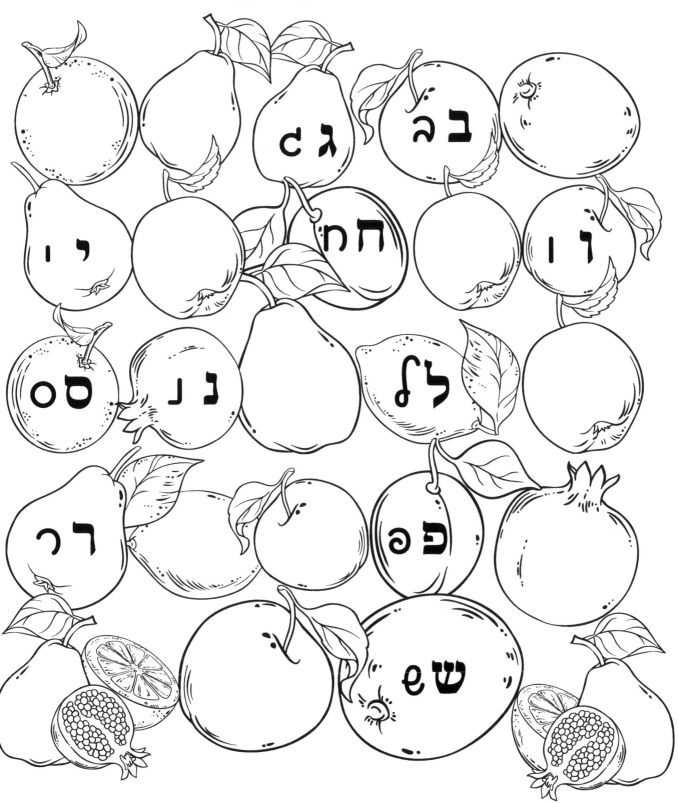

FIND 10 DIFFERENCES

WRITE & DRAW
THE STORY OF EXODUS

Recreate the Hebrews' story from the moment the pharaoh chose to enslave the Jewish people, through Moshe's encounter with God, multiple visits to the pharaoh, plagues, and - finally - living Egypt behind.

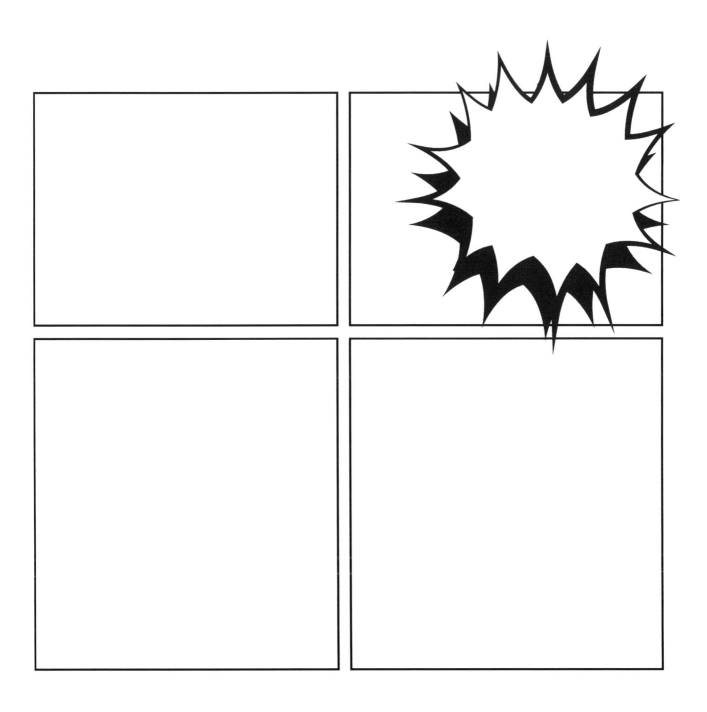

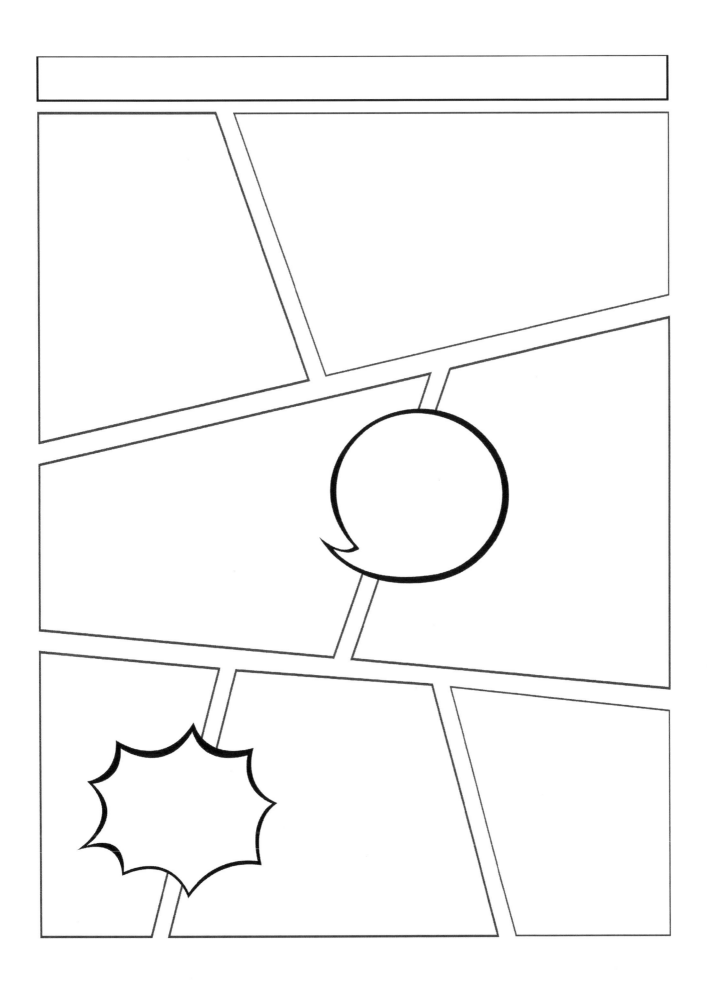

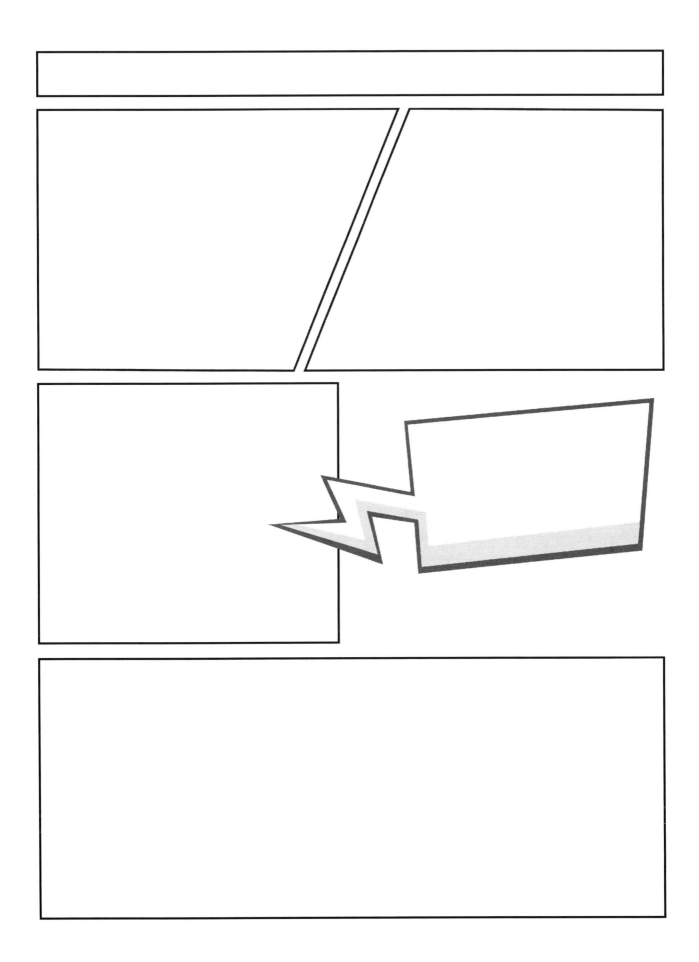

TORAH VERSES WORTH KNOWING

אֲנִי ה' וְהוֹצֵאתִי אֶתְכֶם מִתַּחַת סִבְלֹת מִצְרַיִם וְהִצַּלְתִּי אֶתְכֶם מֵעֲבֹדָתָם וְגָאַלְתִּי אֶתְכֶם בִּזְרוֹעַ נְטוּיָה וּבִשְׁפָטִים גְּדֹלִים:

I am LORD. I will bring you out from under the burdens of Egypt, and I will save you from their slavery. I will redeem you with an outstretched arm, and with acts of great judgments.

אני ה' והוצאתי אתכם

מתחת סבלת מצרים

והצלתי אתכם מעבדתם

וגאלתי אתכם בזרוע נטויה

ובשפטים גדלים

PESACH WORDSEARCH

```
M I R I A M E G Y P T I A N S V O
F C T P U X X K S L T G J U X A H
B D L X H M O S H E G F C V P A F
M P J M A P A S S O V E R D S C S
H L R X U G V P S T C E J E G U Y
K T F V H S E M E X O D U S A N A
G U N P A L K H H H B R J V C G D
D K D X I U A T G O L S A P H N I
Q F J J N D D B F A W H P H O S L
W R A Q A P X N U R J S F R L K O
Z H I G S Y Y Y K A K Z A A I Y H
M G G P I B H T X H F H V E Q N O
I A W E N C A O J P A E O Q M X G
H M D S R E D E S S R Q L Q B Y B
W C I A P V N E X Y W K U U C V E
K Z V C X D P Q V Z T E M A H C D
Q E H H R T Q Q Q J E S H E M O T
```

slavery Elijah exodus Shemot Torah spring Nisan
holidays chametz Haggadah Seder Passover Pesach
Miriam Aharon Moshe pharaoh Egyptians

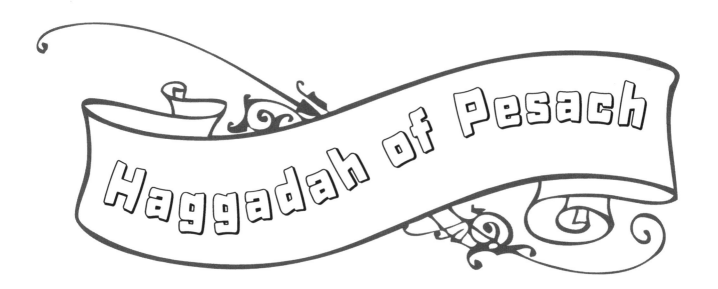

Haggadah of Pesach

הגדה של פסח

PESACH IN A MAZE

Avigail, Daniel, Benji, and Rut can't wait to celebrate Pesach!
But first, they have to find all the chometz!
Help them find it before Pesach starts!

MY OWN HAGGADAH

Design the cover for your own Haggadah!

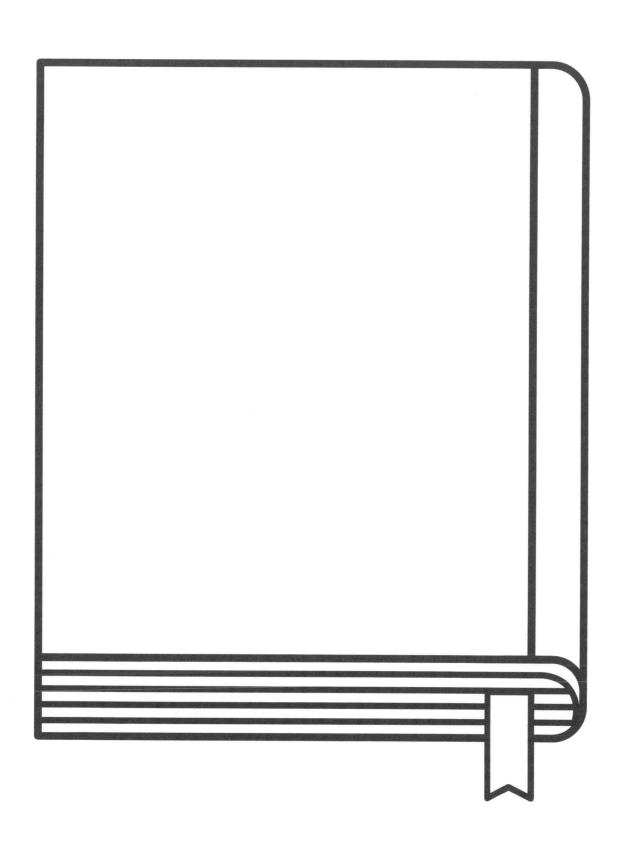

THE SEDER OF THE SEDER

The Hebrew word "seder" means an order. On that night we follow the traditional order of things. Match the Hebrew names with their English transliterations by coloring pairs the same color.

MAGGID

וּרְחַץ

קַדֵּשׁ

YACHATZ

נִרְצָה

BAREICH

כּוֹרֵךְ

TZAFUN

כַּרְפַּס

KADEISH

NIRTZAH

הַלֵּל

רָחְצָה

צָפוּן

MOTZI MATZAH

מָרוֹר

SHULCHAN OREICH

KARPAS

יַחַץ

HALLEL

בָּרֵךְ

MAROR

שֻׁלְחָן עוֹרֵךְ

URCHATZ

מַגִּיד

RACHTZAH

KOREICH

מוֹצִיא מַצָּה

THE SEDER OF THE SEDER

So many stages! It's important to know what we do.
Draw an image illustrating each stop of the Seder night:

KADESH

URCHATZ

KARPAS

YACHATZ

MAGID

RACHTZAH

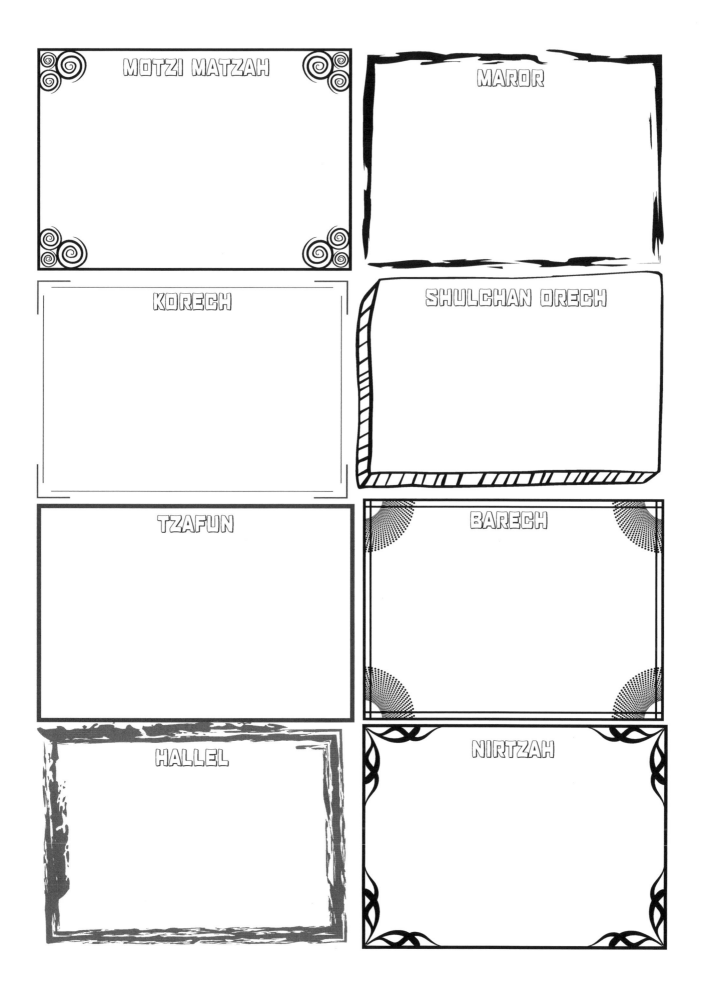

MOTZI MATZAH

MAROR

KORECH

SHULCHAN ORECH

TZAFUN

BARECH

HALLEL

NIRTZAH

PESACH WORDSEARCH

```
P G K Z P M U K Z T A H C R U I Y
N U R O A D A N A H I C D N I P S
J P N G R D S I N A U E N N Y O H
A K G J E E N Q R Z H R K I I Q U
V I T I F L I F O T V O K S N K L
D W S X J U B C C A X K K W Z W C
I H E R S V A R H M S I V N K J H
V J N J O Y S B T I H A C X Q F A
W B X O M R H R Z Z C P V H T J N
K Q K J Y R A J A T A M L Y H L O
R T Z A F O N M H O S L K A E J R
X K W H M D N C B M E O Z L S G E
V V B I K Z H T X M P T L S E K C
M T T Y A C H A T Z R A X E Q E H
H V M E B C L E T I H P D D U M N
C K K N X T Z F N C G H A E X O K
K M L P D I P H A M Q I Y R U A V
```

Pesach, Seder, koreich, rochtzah, tzafon, Hallel,
nirtzah, shulchan-orech, korech, maror, motzi-matzah,
maggid, yachatz, urchatz, kadeish

THE 4 EXPRESSIONS OF REDEMPTION

God told the Jewish people in four ways He would save us from Egypt (Exodus 6:6-7). We drink one cup of grape juice (or wine) during the seder meal for each one.

I will bring you out   וְהוֹצֵאתִי

I will save you   וְהִצַּלְתִּי

I will redeem you   וְגָאַלְתִּי

I will take you   וְלָקַחְתִּי

MISSING LETTERS

Josh and Sarah prepare name cards for all the Seder guests in alphabetical order. Please write down the missing letters to help them with the task!

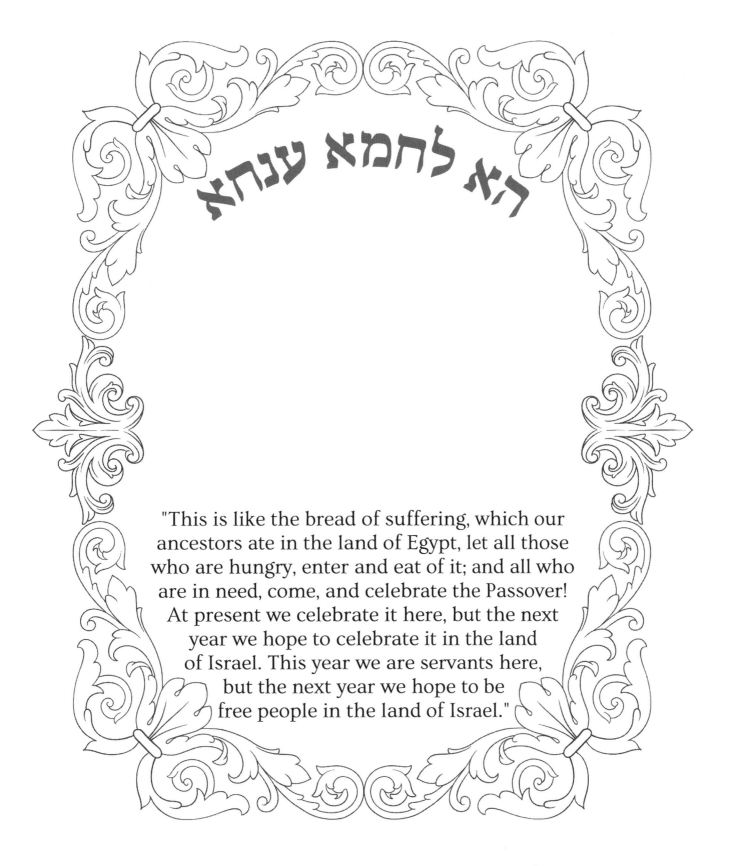

הָא לַחְמָא עַנְיָא

"This is like the bread of suffering, which our ancestors ate in the land of Egypt, let all those who are hungry, enter and eat of it; and all who are in need, come, and celebrate the Passover! At present we celebrate it here, but the next year we hope to celebrate it in the land of Israel. This year we are servants here, but the next year we hope to be free people in the land of Israel."

With the words above we start the 'Maggid' part of Seder. The leader lifts the matzot high so everyone can see it. Illustrate the words of the Haggadah.

מה נשתנה הלילה הזה

What differentiates this night from all other nights?

On all [other] nights we eat
chametz and matzah;
this night, only matsa?

On all [other] nights we eat
other vegetables;
tonight (only) marror.

On all [other] nights, we don't dip
[our food], even one time;
tonight [we dip it] twice.

On [all] other nights, we eat either
sitting or reclining;
tonight we all recline.

Draw illustrations for each of the "Four Questions"

COLORFUL BALAGAN!

Color the Hebrew letters by the instructions below

Lamed - dark red ל
Mem - dark green מ
Nun - light blue נ
Samech - pink ס
Ayin - dark orange ע
Peh - dark blue פ
Tzadi - orange צ
Qof - yellow ק
Resh - light green ר
Shin - red ש
Tav - pink ת

Alef - dark blue א
Bet - light green ב
Gimel - pink ג
Dalet - yellow ד
Hey - purple ה
Vav - light blue ו
Zayin - orange ז
Chet - brown ח
Tet - dark green ט
Yod - red י
Chof - violet כ

עֲבָדִים הָיִינוּ לְפַרְעֹה בְּמִצְרַיִם

We were slaves to Pharaoh in the land of Egypt.
And the Lord, our God, took us out from there with
a strong hand and an outstretched forearm. And if
the Holy One, blessed be He, had not taken our ancestors
from Egypt, behold we and our children and our
children's children would [all] be enslaved
to Pharaoh in Egypt. And even if we were
all sages, all discerning, all elders, all
knowledgeable about the Torah, it
would be a commandment upon us to
tell the story of the exodus from Egypt.
And anyone who adds [and
spends extra time] in telling
the story of the exodus
from Egypt, behold
they are praiseworthy.

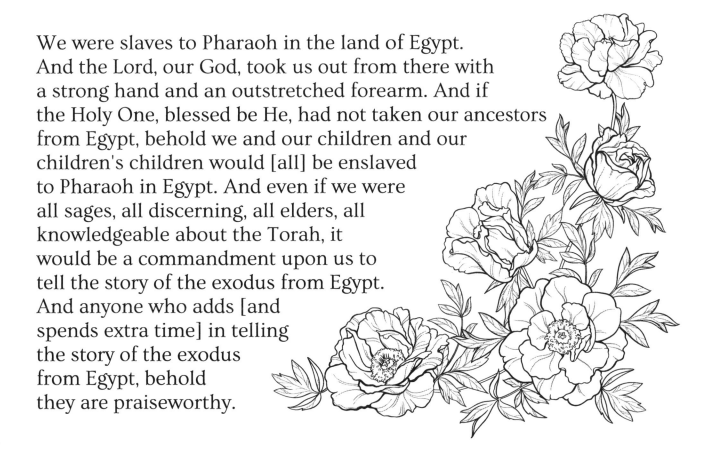

SEDER PLATE

Match the correct Hebrew name with English transliteration
by coloring pairs the same color.

KARPAS

MATZAH

מָרוֹר

זְרוֹעַ

CHAROSET

בֵּיצָה

MAROR

ZEROAH

מַצָּה

חֲזֶרֶת

חֲרוֹסֶת

כַּרְפַּס

BEITZAH

DAYENU!

During the seder night we sing a much loved song called "Dayenu". It expresses the gratitude of the Jewish people for all the wonderful things that God did for us. What are you grateful for? What would your "Dayenu" song be like? Draw and/or write:

_____

_____

_____

_____

_____

_____

_____

_____

_____

PESACH IN NUMBERS

How many of each can you see?

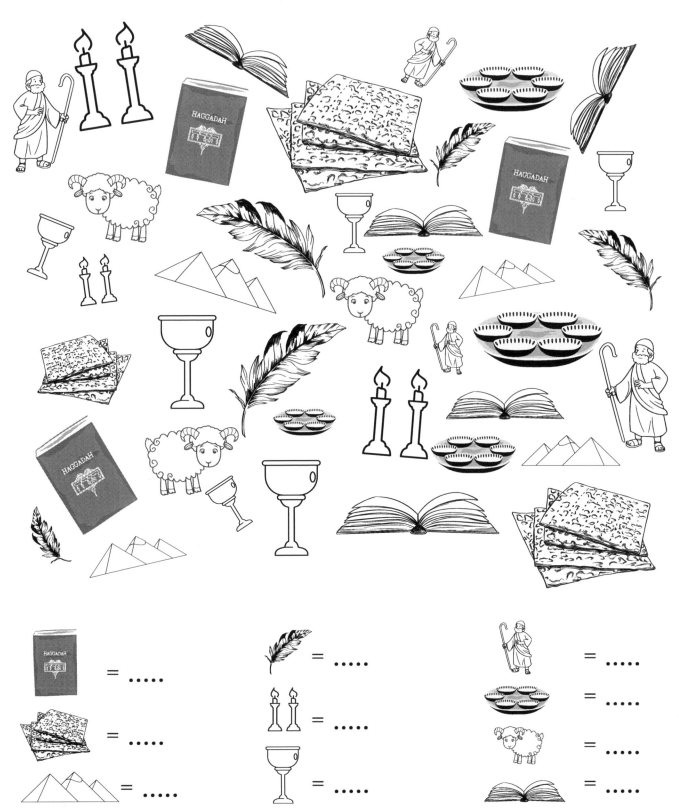

כנגד ארבעה בנים דברה תורה

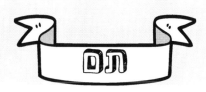

"About four children did the Torah speak;
one [who is] wise, one [who is] wicked, one who is innocent,
and one who doesn't know to ask."

SECRET CODE - IN HEBREW!

Match images with the letters to decode the phrases:

....

   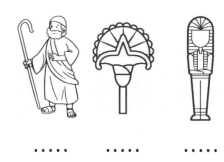

....

SEDER PLATE

Match the English name and food with each of the special items we need to place on our Seder plates. Watch out! There are some impostors trying to get it!

ZEROAH/SHANK BONE

MAROR/BITTER HERBS

DESSERT

BEITZAH/EGG

CHAZERET/ GREENS

MATZAH

KIDDUSH

MITZ/JUICE

CHAROSET

KARPAS/GREENS

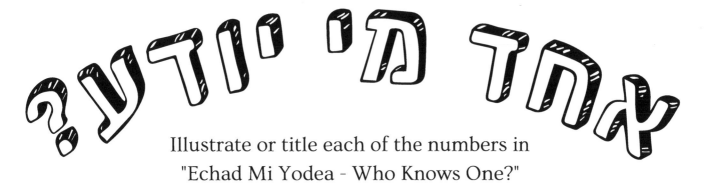

Illustrate or title each of the numbers in
"Echad Mi Yodea - Who Knows One?"

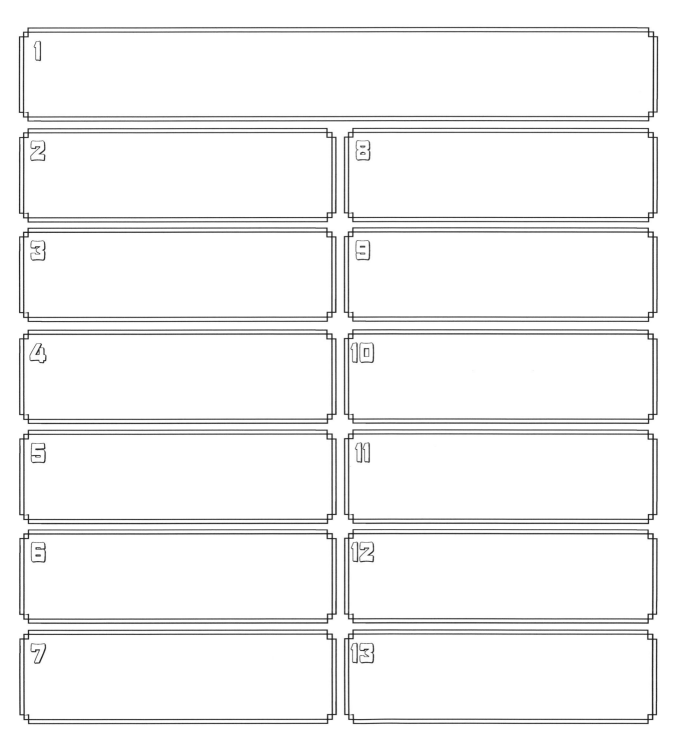

MIRIAM'S CUP

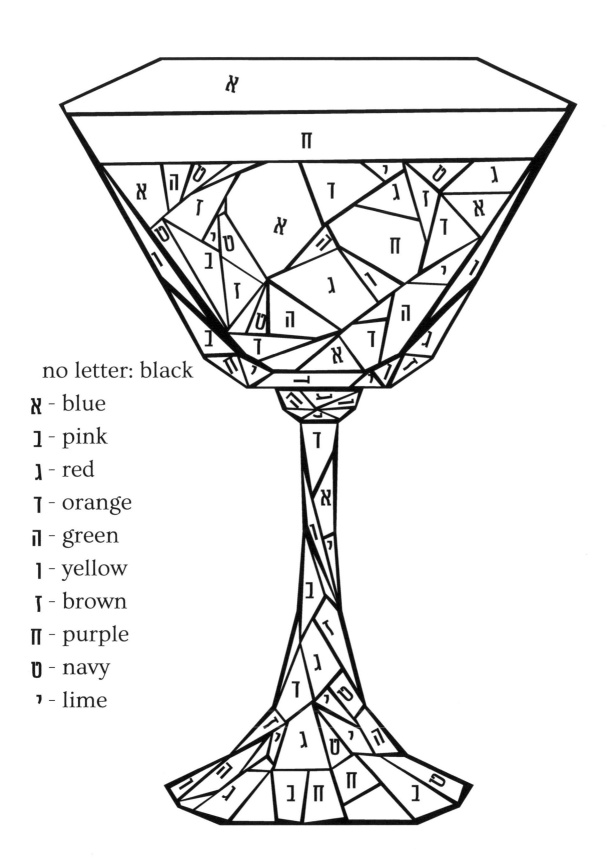

no letter: black

א - blue

ב - pink

ג - red

ד - orange

ה - green

ו - yellow

ז - brown

ח - purple

ט - navy

י - lime

PESACH IN COLOR

Color only the images related to the holiday of Pesach

UNSCRUMBLE THE WORDS!

1. ALEHLL _____

2. ERESD _____

3. TZYAHAC _____

4. OPVSERSA _____

5. INNGSGI _____

6. OARHAHP _____

7. TEOASCRH _____

8. AOFNMIAK _____

9. ELAUSGP _____

10. AOARHN _____

11. ZATHAM _____

12. DSROHAESHIR _____

13. DGAAGAHH _____

14. HEMOS _____

15. SANNI _____

16. IEAHSDK _____

17. HRAZUTC _____

18. OSEDUX _____

19. VRALYES _____

20. NLSHHAUC CRHOE _____

21. HMTEOS _____

22. TEYIATYZ RMITIMAZY _____

23. ODFERME _____

24. A'LHEJSI CUP _____

25. MR'SIAMI UCP _____

26. BATDIK ZHTACEM _____

חד גדיא

Color only the images of characters
mentioned in the song "Chad Gadya"

PESACH CROSSWORD

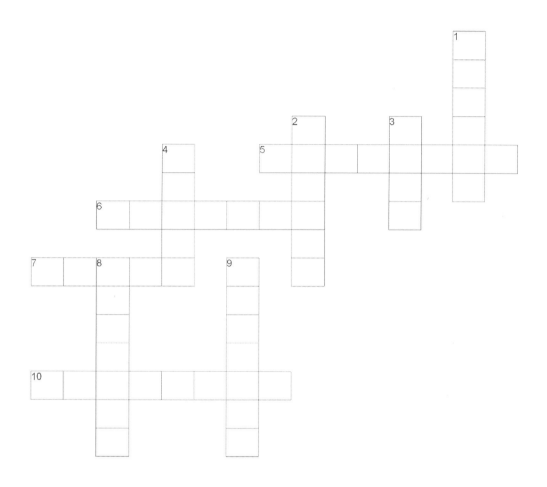

Across:

5
6
7
10

Down:

1
2
3
4
8
9

SECRET CODE - IN ENGLISH

Match images with the letters to decode the words:

   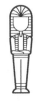

....

....

....

 = e   = l   = r   = s   = a

 = i   = m   = j   = k   = d

 = y   = t   = u   = x   = n

AT MY DREAM SEDER TABLE

If you could invite anyone to your Pesach table - what would your seder dinner look like? Draw it below.